Been There!
SOUTH AFRICA

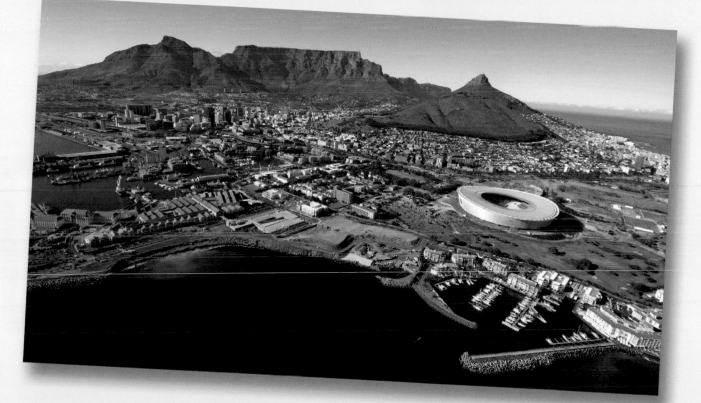

by Annabel Savery

Smart Apple Media

Facts about South Africa

Population: 47 million

Capital Cities: Pretoria, Cape Town, Bloemfontein

Currency: Rand (R)

Main Languages: Afrikaans, English, isiNdebele, isiZulu (and many more!)

Rivers: Orange, Vaal, Limpopo

Area: 470,693 square miles (1,219,090 sq km)

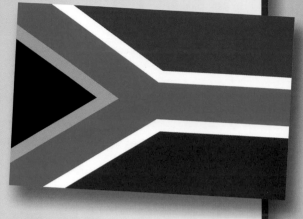

Published by Smart Apple Media
P.O. Box 3263, Mankato, Minnesota 56002

Printed in the United States of America at Corporate Graphics, in North Mankato, Minnesota.

Library of Congress Cataloging-in-Publication Data
Savery, Annabel.
  South Africa / by Annabel Savery.
     p. cm. -- (Been there!)
  Includes index.
  ISBN 978-1-59920-475-8 (library binding)
  1. South Africa--Juvenile literature. I. Title.
  DT1719.S28 2012
  916.804'67--dc22

                         2010042414

Created by Appleseed Editions, Ltd.
Planning and production by
Discovery Books Limited
www.discoverybooks.net
Designed by Ian Winton
Edited by Annabel Savery
Map artwork by Stefan Chabluk
Picture research by Tom Humphrey

Picture Credits: p7 (Gideon Mendel), p9 (Tom Fox/Dallas Morning News), p16 (Hoberman Collection), p20 (Matthew Ashton/ AMA), p22 bottom (Martin Harvey), p23 (Jonathan Blair), p25 top (Hoberman Collection), p25 bottom (John Hrusa/epa), p26 (Carson Ganci/Design Pics), p27 (Richard T Nowitz); Getty Images: p6 (Eric Nathan), p8 (Neil Overy), pp10-11 (Martin Harvey), p14 (Per-Anders Pettersson/Contributor), p15 main (Clinton Friedman); Istockphoto: title & p24 (Louis Hiemstra), p15 top (FourOaks), p17 (ManoAfrica), p18 (MichaelJung), p22 top (AwieBadenhorst), p29 (jrshein); Photo Library: p13 (P. Narayan), p21 (Peter Brooks), p28 bottom (Tim Hill); Shutterstock: p2 (Michael Roeder), p5 top & p31 (MaxPhoto), p5 bottom (palko72), p12 (MichaelJung), p19 top (Victoria Field), p19 bottom (Leksele), p28 top (David Peta).

Cover photos: Istockphoto: left (ManoAfrica); Shutterstock: main (ShutterVision), right (Abraham Badenhorst).

DAD0046
3-2011

9 8 7 6 5 4 3 2 1

Contents

Off to South Africa!

We are going to South Africa!
This is a country on the
continent of Africa.

You can see the route we take
with the arrows on the map below.

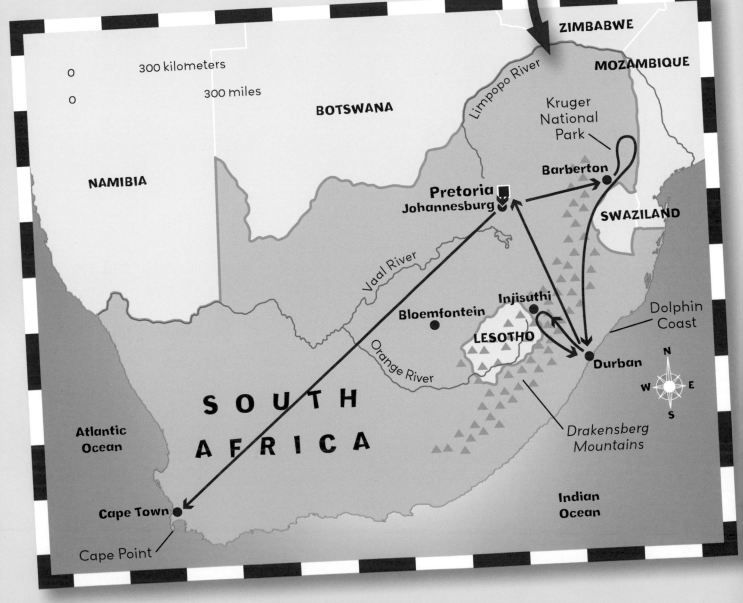

The weather will be mostly warm, but it might also be rainy, so I'll need to take a coat. The west coast is usually cooler than the east coast, and the higher areas are cooler, too. I can't wait to get there!

Here are some things I know about South Africa . . .

- There are lots of wild animals, including giraffes, elephants, and lions. I hope we see some.

- Lots of gold comes from South Africa, as well as other metals and minerals.

- South Africa is called the "rainbow nation." This is because of all the different people who live there.

On our trip, I'm going to find out lots more!

Our plane lands in Johannesburg in the morning. We have all day to explore.

From the airport, we take a taxi to the hotel. The city is very busy. There are many street vendors selling food and souvenirs.

We drive through an area with lots of very tall buildings. The taxi driver says that this is the main business area of the city. He says that lots of people work here.

Outside the city center, there are **suburbs**. Some areas are rich, with big houses. Others are much poorer. These are called townships.

Soweto is one of the townships. We have a guide to show us around. Some parts have nice houses, but in other parts the houses are squeezed together and made from sheets of metal and wood.

The next day, we rent a jeep and drive from Johannesburg to a place called Barberton. We are going to visit a gold mine!

At the gold mine, we each have a dish and have to swirl muddy water in circles to separate the gold from the mud. I can't find any gold, but I still have lots of fun looking!

Gold is found in many places in South Africa. Gold mines go deep underground into the rock. Some can be nearly 3 miles (5 km) deep! Working in a mine is dangerous and very hard work.

The gold industry has brought wealth to South Africa for a long time. However, many mines are closing because they are running out of gold.

Kruger National Park

The next part of our trip is going to be very exciting. We are going on a safari!

We are staying in the Kruger National Park. A national park is an area that is protected by the government. They make sure that animals are not hunted and their **habitats** are not destroyed.

It is fantastic driving through the park. We see lions, leopards, buffalo, and lots of other animals, too.

In the afternoon, we see a herd of elephants crossing a river with their babies. They are amazing!

Exploring Durban

From Kruger National Park, we fly south to the city of Durban. This is the biggest and busiest port in South Africa.

First, we go on a boat tour of the harbor. Huge cargo ships and ferries come and go all day long. There are shiny white yachts and fishing boats on the water, too.

A long time ago, explorers from many different countries, such as Britain, the Netherlands, and India, came to Durban. They brought their building styles and art here. Their **descendants** live in Durban today.

In the afternoon, we go to the Indian district. The Indian district is great to explore. There are busy bazaars and market stalls, as well as the huge Juma Mosque.

At the Beach

Today we all want to go to the beach. We rent a car and travel north from Durban.

There are beaches to the north and south of Durban. Lots of people come here from Johannesburg and other inland cities.

The part of the coast we're going to is known as the Dolphin Coast. Because the water is quite shallow, dolphins live here all year round. I hope we see some.

The sea here is the Indian Ocean. Mom says there are sharks here, too. She says that there are nets in the water to keep them away from swimmers. It's scary swimming when sharks might be nearby!

The sea is lovely and warm. After swimming, we have races up and down the long, sandy beach!

Zulu Village Life

The next morning, we decide to visit a Zulu village. Dad explains that the Zulu are people who have lived in this area for many hundreds of years.

The village is inland from Durban. Zulu traditional houses are shaped like domes. Inside they are quite big and feel cool. The women are wearing beautiful clothes and lots of colored beads, too.

Some of the Zulu people living in South Africa today still follow their traditional way of life. Others live in the cities and wear western dress, like you and me, instead of traditional clothes.

There are some stalls, and one woman is selling clothes made of brightly colored beads.

The Zulu are the biggest **indigenous** group in South Africa, but there are many other groups, too. They all speak different languages.

In the Mountains

From the village, we travel farther inland to the Drakensberg Mountains. The journey takes two hours.

We are staying at a place called Injisuthi. From here, we follow a trail that is very steep and leads up into the hills.

The mountains above us are high, with jagged, rocky tops. We can see one of the highest peaks, called Champagne Castle.

We go to see some rock paintings. They were made 8,000 years ago by people called the San. The San lived in the mountains. The paintings show animals and people. It's amazing how old they are!

There are rushing rivers and waterfalls, too. Eagles and vultures fly above our heads.

A Capital City

After visiting the mountains, we travel back to Durban and then fly to the city of Pretoria.

The heart of Pretoria is Church Square. In the center is a grassy area where lots of people are sitting in the sun. There are important looking buildings all around us.

South Africa has three capital cities. Pretoria is where the president and the cabinet are based, Cape Town is the where the parliament is located, and Bloemfontein is where the **Supreme Court** is. How confusing!

In the evening, we go to a restaurant for dinner. I have *boerewors*. This is a kind of sausage made with meat and spices, and it is rolled into a coil. It's delicious.

The *boerewors* is cooked on a barbecue called a *braai*. Braais are very popular in South Africa.

On the Train

From Pretoria, we travel back to Johannesburg to catch a train to Cape Town. We leave at 10:30 a.m. and will arrive in Cape Town at lunchtime tomorrow.

We pass through farmland where crops such as sugarcane and corn are growing. Vineyards are planted in straight rows. People are busy working here.

Early the next morning, we travel through the Great Karoo. This is an enormous area of dry, flat grasslands, or plains. It covers about 154,440 square miles (400,000 sq km) of land.

"Karoo" means "land of great thirst." Although the area is dry, many types of plants and wildlife live here.

Arriving in Cape Town

When we arrive in Cape Town, it is hot and sunny.

Table Mountain towers above the city. There are two other hills, too: Lion's Head and Devil's Peak. They act like the sides of a bowl with the city in the middle.

Devil's Peak

Table Mountain

Lion's Head

From the city center, we take a bus to the Victoria and Alfred Waterfront. There are all sorts of boats in the harbor and lots of places to shop and to eat.

We catch a boat from the waterfront to Robben Island. There is a big building on the island. It was a prison and is now a museum. People who were against apartheid were imprisoned here. One of them was Nelson Mandela.

Nelson Mandela later became president of South Africa. In 1993, he was awarded the Nobel Peace Prize.

Up to Table Mountain

It is a lovely, clear day, so we take a cable car to the top of Table Mountain. The cable car is shaped like a fishbowl, and it turns as we go up so that we can see all around.

From the top, we can see all over Cape Town. From up here, the boats moving around the waterfront look tiny.

Back in the city, we walk along Adderley Street. This is one of the main shopping streets. There is a market selling lots of handicrafts and clothes, and there is also a flower market.

We all buy souvenirs to take home with us. Mom and I buy some colorful beads. They will remind me of our trip to South Africa.

A Fun Last Day

To the south of the city is the Cape Peninsula. This is a piece of land that stretches into the ocean. At the tip are two points, the Cape of Good Hope and Cape Point. This is where we are going today.

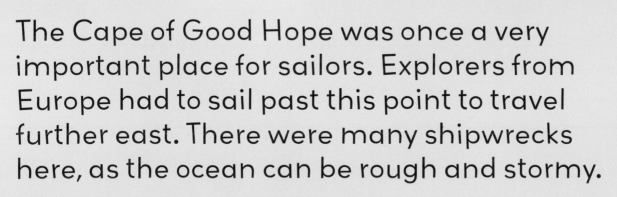

The Cape of Good Hope was once a very important place for sailors. Explorers from Europe had to sail past this point to travel further east. There were many shipwrecks here, as the ocean can be rough and stormy.

On the way back to the city, we stop at Boulders Beach. There is a penguin **colony** here. We have lots of fun watching them waddle around!

In the evening, we go to a restaurant for our last meal in South Africa. I have *bobotie*. This is a dish with spicy beef on the bottom and egg custard on the top. Yum!

After dinner, we pack for our journey home tomorrow. I have had a great time on our trip to South Africa!

My First Words in IsiZulu

There are 11 official languages in South Africa. isiZulu, isiNdebele, and Afrikaans are the most common. Here are some phrases in isiZulu to get you started.

Sawubona (*say* **Sawoo-boh-nah**) Hello

Hamba kahle
(*say* **Ham-bah gah-shle**) Goodbye

Unjani? (*say* **Oon-jah-nee?**) How are you?

Ngubani igama lakho?
(*say* **Ngoo-bah-nee ee-gah-mah lah-khoh?**) Thank you

Igama lami ngu Sam.
(*say* **Ee-gah-mah la-mee ngoo Sam**) My name is Sam.

Counting 1 to 10

1 **kunye**   (**koo-nyay**)
2 **kubili**   (**koo-billy**)
3 **kuthathu** (**koo-thah-thu**)
4 **kune**   (**koo-nay**)
5 **kuhlanu** (**koo-lah-noo**)
6 **yisithupa** (**yee-see-too-pah**)
7 **yisikhombisa**
   (**yee-see-kom-bee-sah**)

8 **yisishiyagolombili**
   (**yee-see-shee-ah-gah-lom-billy**)

9 **yisishiyagalolunye**
   (**yee-see-shee-ah-gah-low-loo-nyay**)

10 **yishumi** (**yee-shoo-mee**)

Words to Remember

apartheid a system where people of different colors or races have to live separately

cabinet a group of officials who give advice to the head of a government

colony a group of animals of the same type living together

descendants people who are the family of people who lived a long time ago

habitat the natural environment of an animal or plant

indigenous people who originally come from a place

Nobel Peace Prize a prize given every year to a person or organization that has worked toward peace between or within countries

parliament a group of people who make the laws for a country

plains wide, flat areas of land

Supreme Court the highest law court in the country

suburbs the area surrounding a town or city

Index

Learning More about South Africa

Books

Discover South Africa (Discover Countries) Chris Ward, PowerKids Press, 2010.
Focus on South Africa (World in Focus) Jen Green, World Almanac Library, 2007.
In South Africa (Global Adventures) Judith Mazzeo Zocchi, Dingles & Co, 2008.
South Africa (Countries in the News) Michael Gallagher, Smart Apple Media,
    2008.

Web Sites

Geography for Kids, Geography Online, and Geography Games
    http://www.kidsgeo.com/index.php
National Geographic Kids, People & Places
    http://kids.nationalgeographic.com/kids/places/find/south-africa
SuperKids Geography directory, lots of sites to help with geography learning
    http://www.super-kids.com/geography.html